on generation & corruption

Poets Out Loud

Elisabeth Frost, series editor

on
generation
&
corruption

poems

Terrence Chiusano

Fordham University Press   NEW YORK   2015

Fordham University Press has no responsibility for the
persistence or accuracy of URLs for external or third-
party Internet websites referred to in this publication
and does not guarantee that any content on such
websites is, or will remain, accurate or appropriate.

Fordham University Press also publishes its books
in a variety of electronic formats. Some content that
appears in print may not be available in electronic
books.

Visit us online at www.fordhampress.com.

Library of Congress Control Number: 2014952820

Printed in the United States of America

17 16 15 5 4 3 2 1

First edition

. . . the question might be raised whether substance (i.e. the 'this') comes-to-be at all. Is it not rather the 'such,' the 'so great' or the 'somewhere,' which comes to be?

—Aristotle, *On Generation and Corruption* (I.3, 317b20–25)

From one to two,
is the first rule.

—Robert Creeley, from "Gemini"

How strange. A disaster occurs and still a man notices a picture.

—Vladimir Nabokov, *Laughter in the Dark*

contents

acknowledgments

Early versions of some of these poems, whole or in fragments, and often with different titles, have appeared in *Basinski: A 'Zine of the Arts*; *Can We Have Our Ball Back?*; *Ignation*; *Ixnay*; *Kenning: A Newsletter of Contemporary Poetry, Poetics, and Nonfiction Writing*; *Mirage #4/Period(ical)*; *Queen Street Quarterly: Forum for the Contemporary Canadian Arts*; *Serving_Suggestion*; and *trifectapress*.

Versions of two portions of "Stunts and Forfeits" appeared as individual Buffalo Vortex broadsides (Buffalo Vortex, Dec. 2000). A version of parts one and two of "Some Off-light," together with a version of "Finishing Work on the Face, Left Arm and Foot," appeared as a $ellsheets e-broadside (The $ellsheets, Jun. 2004).

An early version of parts one and two of the present work was published in an unbound, limited edition chapbook of 221 copies under the title *On Generation and Corruption: Parts I and II* (Buffalo NY: Handwritten Press, 2003).

The cover image was created using GigaPan® technology and may be viewed at http://www.gigapan.com/gigapans/43806. I thank Dror Yaron for his assistance.

start

agenda box

There is no intimate between *me* and *my*. But there is between *appearance*. And this is the coin, as the saying is. What's given for the coin is counted and cross-counted, grouped into "right determinations" like colors on a wheel. *How loyal is your palette?* is the question begged by a certainty so certain, so tight and shiny and stubbornly shut, its sparkle of honesty, its halo of fact, is more fiercely a glow, but aglow more falsely, than any other judgment of our fealty on whose mercy we also fear we're thrown, on whose rack we're redeemed or broken, on whose grass like goats we're starved or grown. But every intimate depends on this: to balk at right determinations, at treacheries of stubbornness, at cross-counts and lists, to beg for something different—the actual, the sincere sight. But why?

Go. Listen. Observe. And remember: the touch touches but luck helps things sound good. So forgive the quick peeks that passed for answers, the flinches that passed for pointing, the fumbling figments that passed my lips like the bleats of a lost sheep; forgive the scrape the stiff door makes, stiff because the shadow of the calamity falls the length of every floor. Not by portraiture, not by a spitting image or a perfect likeness, not by semblance will the canoe that carries us be made, but by parable, motto, proverb, rumor, fable, gossip, gab—not without finesse, not without flex of pace and texture too, and more, yes—but even so, it may never reach the safety of the fading shore before obscuring its own sight.

If *between* is the revealing beam, the revealing ray of light, if *me* is a string and two tin cans, *my* a pipette pulling through its little tube one line at a time, if *appearance* is mossy and plush and moldable (wet turf taking stiff thumb), vacant but somehow plural, barren but shaped in funny ways (from knots and cuppings and dimples to deeply bent doglegs, from snow-swept prairies to sunny hay-fields and cozy hedge-rows), if *hearing* is hearing the off-kilter suites (the overloaded lines, misfired canons, mis-keyed medleys, the overloaded rhymes) as only one small part of only one kind of partial chart, if *the verticals* are "vertical" in the sense that an inclined plane is some-times shaped like a corkscrew, then what's actually chronicled isn't the sound inside the beaten gong or the motor inside the moving mouth, nor is it the sight of *the actual* or *the sincere*, what's chronicled is the view viewed from near then far, the creep the vista seems seduced to make, its *here* partitioned from its *there* as if a hair pulled from a head. It's true, it may read like flung mud, but if I've treed it just so—barked it up a lofty elm or aspen, graphed it with a fleet of neatly interlocking lemmas—what's actually chronicled is the muddening of the made view, the way appearance seems to bewitch and summon to itself an entire bevy of *intimates* and *betweens*.

one

It ought to open like a peacock's tail—many-eyed, marbled, feathery, fanned—instead of a can of baked beans opened onto a kitchen counter. It ought to travel a circuit as exact and merciless as a millstone's grinding meal, coil into a curve as precise as a woodland turd pinched onto a patch of pale green lichen. Instead, from either side the other side seems higher, from either end the opposite end. The freckling, so it seems, isn't fixed— but isn't thereby fitful or blind or fouled like a miscast fishing line. It's as if something moistened, loosened, slipped, came unknit; the last knot in a long tether, the last strand of a resisting net. It's as if I didn't already know, as if I'd eavesdropped on a little crowd at a booth in a bar, as if I'd only *overheard*, as if I'd never been here before, never gathered pebbles from a slender beach beside a sharp bend in a shallow river, never slogged through marsh grass and mud holes, picked my way through thickets of jaggers, groves of wild grape, never dozed in the shade of a cottonwood, peed on a pine stump, barked my shin on the knot of a fallen willow, never climbed over a stone fence into the sun of a summer-mown hay-field nor worked my way through a knob of ash and scrub oak, a meadow of bluegrass and clover, through the crown of oleander circling the hilltop manor,

its croquet yard, slate walks, cemetery, granite veranda, never waited for nightfall in a thicket of forsythia, never snuck into the garden shed you'd left unlocked to gather rope and shears, fill a sock with pebbles and lead shot, hide the hatchet in a bale of rags, pry the pick head from its handle . . . spill the can of gas. Let's assume the track

has a back (hard to, but we must), the glare an instability, the bottom a top soft and black. As for the pushing let's say the preserving takes its place, for the periodic the permanent, for the piling the pull . . . as if for a bean its green sprout, for a speckled trout its clear stream, for the knock the knees when fear fills them with doubt.

For the joke, let's imagine I see myself leaving but I can't hear what I say as I go. As for the page, let's suppose its lines are a kind of overgrowth, they show me a way to mount—to *that* from *this below*. For the struggle let's pretend it's like the plight of a dull plow plowing a field of frozen stubble, or the sorrows of my troubled foot on its way into my misguided mouth. As for the rest, let's assume it's overridden: tire tracks appearing in place of carriage and cart ruts; a girl and a dog on a dirt bike where there were only hills, fog, firs, rain; dusty side streets where there was deep mud; the heat of summer noon in place of winter's woodstove; where hoof plod and horse huff now boom cars, street rods, jeep-beats. And so the so-called counterstroke arrives, its so-called "canopy of advantage" in tow—its stretchiness "the stretchiness of a rubbery guess," its softness "the softness of spat phlegm" —but little bigger than a thumbhole, little less bland, little fancier with its oblong footwork than a patch of reflected sunlight drifting the destined length of its daylong way from brass-railed sideboard to dining room wall to calfskin lampshade to teak side table to mounted moose head to dim corridor to inlaid doorjamb to the floor of the cork-paneled drawing room halfway down the hall, only to dissolve into oblivion on the corner

of a Persian carpet, there, between the paw of a napping Pekingese and the leg of a red leather davenport, succumbing to the shadows of a summer day's deepening dusk in the midst of a jumble of arabesques, intertwined fishes, flowering vines, peacocks, poppies, pine cone-like palmettes. The phone rings: "francis:

woke at noon to church bells—ate one orange—extinguished fan—stretched—I dreamt of a beautiful garden, of lilacs and cherry trees, of all our friends eating figs and roe, of the sweet filth of those few brutal minutes bent across your mother's open bureau—relax, it's over." If Piranesi's etchings of sets of drawings of views of groups of sets of views redraft the looseness of *the given* into the starched stiffness of a set piece, THE CHEST OF NESTED CHESTS, but are also master meddlers that sift while they settle, relax and fluff while they flatten, that loosen and drive the stiffness of *the given* over the cliff and into the sea of THE HAPHAZARDLY STACKED

then may these do the same, even if the views slur a bit as they slip and skid, as they slide from kitchen table to river basin to forest footpath to rods of bluebells and shafts of bay, from fieldstone fence to granite veranda to garden bench to thickets of thorns and myrtles to slopes of new-baled hay, from bath house to cloakroom

to bedchamber to mastiffs and foxhounds asleep in the grass, from sitting room to porch swing to attic to dovecote to woodshed to a pair of hog-tied wrists decomposing in a bloody bedsheet to ribbons of day-glo surveyor's tape stapled to wooden stakes staked in a circle behind a fallen willow near the steep bank and short beach of a sharp bend in a shallow river reflecting in its sandy flats a stand of lodgepole pines purpling beneath the July sun setting behind this dusty little border town called B. The wait waits. The wait whistles. The wait wonders. The wait wavers. The wait wishes it would've opened with the grace of a feathery fan (*This is the same house.*

This is a there. I await what's already found.) instead of the urgent spasms of an overfilled bladder. Even so— it may flop like a hooked fish, hiss like a poked tire, wobble and shrivel and weaken and split, but it cakes and thickens too, into a guide as stepped and firmly knowing as a Latin primer, a signpost as primly precise

as little paper apples with little pictures pinned on: F is for a "FRIEND IN NEED"—C is for starting this off with a little "COUGH"—D is for "DEAR FRANCIS: a last-minute message before travel—schedules nonexistent now, dashing place to miserable place—a ringing in my ears . . . I race around looking for a friendly face."

sally ho! a vexing journey, landfall at last

ONE

I was at my going-away party out by
          the county fairgrounds—horsing around
with school pals, downing gin, tossing

horseshoes, clowning with my little cousin
          playing "make-believe" town: *Go past clock*
tower, park bench, past the bakery, butcher,

cobbler, past the barbershop beside the empty
          parking lot, the tramp camped under the train
trestle, past the forests and marshes at the far

edge of town, follow the footpath to the fork
          in the creek. Meet me behind the fallen tree.
It's getting dark. I'm getting drunk. I need

to pee. So there I am *there I aming*, bored,
          staring through a slit in the shithouse door
and all of a sudden I see her—black hair

in a bob, blue sequined dress, blue pillbox
          hat with a feather and half-veil—floating
over a picnic bench, drifting, flickering

like a vision of The Virgin, floating at me
          over a ditch, a bush, a fence and whispering
all the while, "Look for me one sunny day,

on your way, behind a hedge at the edge
          of a field of hay." She frowns, sighs, waves
her hand, "I shouldn't say that. I should

never betray the end; never divide it; never
          crowd it with the middle of the way." I froze.
I went numb. It was as if I fell into a daze.

TWO

I could only make forty miles that day.
    It was wet, windy, dreary, cold. Real cold.
Sun was setting when I came to an old

fishing-port and sawmill town—filthy little
    main street littered with oyster tins and gull
feathers, strips of bark, bottle caps, mud

puddles, sawdust, pigeon crap—and some
    yokel stumbles up dead drunk: hard hat,
hip waders, check shirt, chinos, lunch box,

buck knife, thick black belt. Both hands
    were bright pink—flaked, blotchy, creased,
wrinkled—bright white and pink and blue.

They'd been burnt once. Bad. His chin,
    cheek, ear, scalp. Part of his neck too. He
asks if I've come a long way, if I'm alone,

if I'm hungry, if I need a place to stay.
    I should've known he was a bad omen
with his bald head and his blank face,

standing there swaying leg-to-leg, reeking
    of diesel and dead fish, staring down my
shirt, bleeding from a cut knuckle, offering

a pint of gin, shivering from the wind
    and the drink and the wet, sun setting
hard behind his head, hard and fast,

flattening the tree tops, caving-in the tide
    flats, caving-in the top of every last dirty
little shop like the lid of a casket closing.

THREE

They told me to look for the slums north
            of town. Somehow I ended up somewhere
south instead (there was a storm kicking

up, I was frantic, cutting through rose beds
            and herb gardens, jumping fences, hopping
hedges, bird baths, lawn statues, whatever

was in my way, and that day it seemed
            like every pebble in the world was, every
green blade of grass) and there I stood,

near the old mill, at the little crossroads
            between the hollows and the heights—lost,
worried, winded—and damned if I know

why but down into The Corners I go.
            It's cramped and dark from the narrow
streets, the heat, the hills, the gathering

clouds, the crows, the blowing trees—but
            the whole place seems empty. No cars, no
kids, no moms, dads, dogs, cats. Nothing

but row after deserted row of rickety
            bungalows and clapboard shacks. And
I'm standing there, looking around,

scratching my head, wondering *what's*
            next (there a boarded window—tarped
hedges . . . there a smashed mailbox—

baseball bat—overturned apple cart—
            lawn speared with lawn darts)—suddenly
there's a hand on the back of my neck.

i

Two lines of nine stand face-to-face, turn in rank to face forward, peel off and parade one-by-one down the center (first-from-right, first-from-left, second-from-right, second-from-left, third-from-right . . . and so on), then at the other end they cross or curl as the case may be (first-from-right to left, first-from-left to right, second-from-right to right, second-from-left to left, third-from-right to left . . . and so on), until they gather once more into two lines of nine to start the figure anew. Then they go, and go again, until it ends when the first two lines of nine stand face-to-face.

stunts and forfeits

1

If the new is not shiny,
if the string is by design trebled and the line
thus made mid, if the vale is stretched like a tendon
end to dreary end
and by use overworn, if the roll rolls back and they
say *let it hover never mind*
the tugs to one side or another, if the shaft is mine
and the ring I've rung
to remind is slipping, if a name veers but another
follows in its pocket,
if a line, as I've said, is made mid, if the light I catch
I catch to keep the lock

2

it makes from keeping
step with keeping kept, if perpetual
change is the chase in exchange for caring what's
caught . . . I see the dock
spread to meet its junction—box, as the box halves
itself, that the fin is pulled
through water by wheel-and-string. I see the scene
much as I see my
cleft-in-chin (sunny, welcome, warm) but when I see
the river it's droughted,
logs jammed at the fork. I see the little oxbow bend,
its short beach and steep

3

bank white with bird
shit. I see "the close" as rows of shabby
brick homes, "the small" as "yards next to." I see
the cankers: the splintered
hay rakes and rusting harrows, the parched farms,
fallow fields, the high
school built near a dirt track, the dark little woodlots,
the sandlots, flooded
quarries, the dark little hearts. I feel the woe descend
like a plague. I hear
the parlor full of strangers. I know the priors involve
who and *where*. I see

4

the sinister, the deceptive.
I see the end. I say I see the uncertainty—
an honest acceptance, a deficiency pinching a line
at its gut—but I can't say
I see the sight. As for the light, I hem but do I haw?
"Her hips, dear ladies
and gents, are as round and firm as a pair of curling
stones but as chaste
as a widow at a Sunday matinee." And so the wing
is shot . . . off . . . maybe clean
off, and shows the river rippling; balance ensembled,
drift held unaccountably

5

in. Right. Pale, sapped,
befuddled, bewildered, spread thin,
I rest, hang my head, take my place, act out yet
another attraction, submit
to a weakness to insist, warm a chair with the seat
of my dungarees because
that's where I think I'm needed, seek a dim corner,
take a long hour, step
out, am gone forever. If I remember you, I remember
you *still* but I remember
you *again*. The variation might be small—a barely
balanced ensemble

6

of "somehow," a line
footed, its hole limed ahead—but
I repeat it day after day. I repeat: the gesture (*still
and again*) is a hog nosing
its slop-trough, a wet knot worked free, an ointured
thumb pressed into
an open sore, a crescent of discord spread as wide
as the web a giant spider
weaves over its treasured island. A handbook may
here be handy but let's let
it slide into the "merely described" (warm tap beer,
torn seat cushions, worn

7

floorboards, a lovely little
bumpkin of a barkeep fair as a May
rose, a green recruit home on his first leave, a stroll
through our dusty *ville*,
a few turns around the town square, brush of thumb
to cheek, double-time
into the scrub of the low lusty hills, O! the stiff collar,
the quaking shirtsleeve,
O! the hiked skirt, the torn blouse, the burst buttons,
the summer heat, O!
the rotten places you've seen, every in-between, every
alleluya an arch of fear)

8

because the crosshatch,
the work of the crosshatch, is a garland,
a festoon, a spool, a relay made to pattern, to sift
the patterned, to push
as if a pin into its cushion the point of the patterned,
to set aside, to survey
the site. The pitch is blunt: the group of two is one;
the shape is a judge,
the fold in its beak formed by the chase of its own
ass; the way is a forfeit
paid; the effort is a name, an elaborate hoax, a stunt,
a new Jazz Age; the act

9

is an absolute as golden
as a field of frozen wheat but the fact
is so much more than mere timing—a need to bend
for the common good.
I vary—not to release, to keep. To keep telling: white
lacquerware wardrobe,
lone hair caught in door-catch—color of dried reed,
loft straw, corn husk,
rib of an early season maple leaf. That's all. That's it.
The phone rings: "francis:
goddamn this horrible heat! the hordes of houseflies,
my miswired ceiling fans,

10

the sand I can't seem
to shake from my bedsheets, the smell
I can't seem to scrub from my panties—I'm so hot
I nearly stove in my own
head like a depressed Swede—listen closely: today,
near the old mill, I found
a bloody rope and a rusty hatchet, a bloody blanket,
a broken mirror—I hid
them in a hole under a stump—call me . . . call soon."
A book is made to last:
active, borne about, a timing so much more timely
than a billfold full of ticks

11

tocked by an official timer.
Even so, sometimes she's blue as a robin's
egg, blue as the little boy with his bugle fast asleep
beneath the haystack—
consumed by loneliness, homesickness, postponed
by fear, hate, envy, dread.
But it'd take more than a few lousy little lines of *nein!*
to overwhelm her telltale
too-readiness to force the tone; it'd take more than
a wolf in sheep's clothes.
So let's say someone at a party suddenly says, "I'm
thinking of a word that

12

rhymes with . . . *cake.*"
Someone replies, "Is it a tool to gather up
hay?" The asker of the riddle will say, "No. It's not
a rake." And so on, until
the answer is given. And by such division, as it daily
partitions me, grins me
ear to toe, I'm ticked like a clock: head well up, eyes
forward but face gloppy,
brain clotted . . . hair a matted mess. Fuck. I'm stuck.
Choosing is choosing
which to skip, which *from this*, which center, is ready
and set to find its furthest

13

shore. Thus the heap
is loosened; thus I give wait instead
of chase, and when I'm there, when all are, every
last one, the hold
on the heap is loosened and the looseness of the heap
is by hand honked, is by
hand lessened, and lessoned just the same: that like
an open gate, a turn made
unable to keep its turn is there to wheel a covered
wagon through. The need
is the need to need the need to need back its original
want, to catch until caught.

14

If a stunt is a difficulty
played for fun, and a forfeit a penalty
for making a foul, what then? what's hiding? My
house is still dividing:
three plots widely mooded but equally ballooning—
from clean to dirty, kitsch
to slapstick, old to new—each with its own cue. It's
true, I'm screwed. Imagine
the land is as onerous as it is generous: a tract salty,
marshy, narrow, mean
extending a welcome warmer than sun. Imagine
that if I write I repeat:

15

that if there are limits
they're screened; that if "it" follows
"that if," "follows" follows; that the flicker may
flicker between *impasto,*
rubato, andante, accelerando, largo, legato—each tick
timed by two tiny tocks—
but that the "sock" is back up to its opening always
rerolled, its shape showing
the-laid-out-for, the-already-came; that what was once
a proud and strutting cock
is now beheaded, plucked, gutted, deboned . . . ready
for the family pot. I take

16

sides, certain one's bigger
but stoppable still, and so my luck
is tried. THE STAND thus made may be slack (a guess
is good when it goes home
with me) but its loll may still be collared and dragged.
So it goes 'round—
numbered. But if I stitch I tear too, and if what's torn
is a sheet imagine each
piece is a place for a letter. If I seem in a rush to leave,
I am—because to stay
is to decide (height of reveal? depth of base? breadth
of midline? length of shin

17

shown? tufts, ruffs,
plaits, pleats, plies? does the lid lift
now? should I make a divot where the outside comes
in?), is to do what it takes
to resume, to once more and always choose anew;
is to say that if "want"
is a room-in-waiting then I want two: one to recite
from (even if not *all*, not
quite), one for a maze of foggy phrases, a bedlam
of *why*, *how* and *who*.
And so for our story: If there's division, it chastens.
If there are degrees,

18

they're cajoled—a bag
of mixed nuts spilled and mounded *thus*.
If it's a county fair, it must be corrupt—its innocent
fun defrauded by deceit,
scam, bunkum, flimflam. If there's pastiche or parody,
lampoon, a spoof, a cento . . .
no. It only sounds this way because my doubting pen
chatters as wildly
as the staves of a barrel on its way over The Falls. (*Sa-
aaave meeeeee!*) If I throw
my hat in the ring, I bake my brittle batch. I snap.
If there's a town, I've won.

ii

Two lines of nine stand face-to-face. First three on left form tube, first three on right form tuck, second three on left leap over tuck and return, second three on right thrust through tube, last third on left make flection, last third on right mince, make braid. The figure repeats in reverse—mincers uncrimp, form tube; flectors unflex, form tuck; thrusters leap over tuck and return; leapers thrust through tube; tuckers unpucker, make flection; tubers unfuse, make braid—then it repeats once again until it ends when two lines of nine stand face-to-face.

a parlor full of strangers

ONE

*A bead is drawn on a group in a crowd at the county fairgrounds. Late
summer. Sunday noon. Sky low, ragged, mean. The bead "assembles"
(one* RV, *asphalt lot, three lawn chairs, two trees, tent, ice chest, picnic*

*bench), the group "appoints," crowd tightens its suddenly slipping grip.
The darkness of the slowly darkening day, sensed as much as seen,
weakens the resolve of the leave-taking, deepens the dismay, taints*

*the well-wishing, taints the poor departing girl's felt fate with the image
of a watery grave.* It's bizarre, the whole thing. Laughable. Can't be
evenly lit: the pockmarks, the throngs, balled fists, the glyphs, the lists.

A face lifts: "Yes?" Everything hinges on the surrey with the fringe
on top, the *you* in *them*—the assemblies, appointments, the gloomy
grip—the *you with* that repeats between the *you* and the fractious *from*

a stonecutter's sense of foreshorten-in-relief blended with a painterly
through-to sense of *fore, back* and *middle*; a mesh, a weave, a grain
so old it can't be evenly split, and that daily taken (as the *fict-* for *-ion*,

the *fact-* for *-ure*, the love of "program"—a *fides* full and daily felt)
is a mix so pure that if it counts (front-to-back, side-to-slippery-side)
is an arm, and what it counts is an arm laboring to hide in its hole.

TWO

"francis: coming to B., passing hay-fields and hog farms, july 19, break
of day (my returning to you returning)—let's say hello again, laugh,
kiss, whisper in one another's ear, let's meet again on that little garden

path—I want to hear your voice like a ring on every finger—what
honesty! romance! loyalty! what a chameleon! what a ghost!—I'll never
tire of saying it: we're two coats cut from the same cloth—remember

when we said let's say what we say as if spinning a plate on a spindle
playing a game of 'no regrets'?—you flimpfed it indeedy, muffed it
plain as corn cakes—see? my foot's in the foreground, in the stream

(I'm kneeling in a bed of reeds, bleeding on a fallen fir), and if you
must know the agenda "inside the box": the bigger the shoe the better
to kick you with—P.S. we played games, sure as shit (oh you rotten

scoundrel! you rake! you heartless heel!), but no, the claim was never
made through the local office—P.P.S. THE MAJOR isn't significant,
hardly, he's a nitwit, a toad, buffoon, a sniveling clown of a sore loser

half-crippled by the paddlings he begs me to beat into his wrinkled old
rump cheeks—how he blushes at the sight of his tawdry little tartlet!
how he shivers like a lost lamb! as sure a cad as ever earned his yoke."

THREE

Unhappy hearts may be plumbed like a plum cut to its stone, night-
ghouls may hound us, but verse always goes hollow deep in its cups.
My deepening disgust: when designed to sound like it hasn't. *We*

hardly know our own need. Should I be proud of such intimacies?
The middle of the matter: when *end* is *beginning again.* And the matter
is a matter of motive, so be it, but of method and motif too. And thus

the matter is made. But if the reader objects and clamors for the town
to pinch itself awake ("It's been doused! It's been flattened and worn
like a sandwich board . . . its depths dim, ends dead, cupboards bare!"),

if what's said (the-spindle-and-the-wildly-spinning-plate) is as ready
to bind or subject or limit as it is to loosen and coax free (too deeply
set in its odd and wobbly ways to ever attempt less than both at once),

if it seems like a merry month of sight-seeing was traded for the labors
of a do-it-yerself dig, the wheat for its chaff, the patch for the hole
in its raggedy pants, if every word bristles with doubt, why not presume

the problems have value? (They're not *added*—like spokes to a wheel
for show.) But they needn't be sung like a sacred hymn or recited like
a cycle of North Sea sagas to badger us into believing they have value.

two

daybook

JULY 1

Bog. Spillway. River bank. Cow shit. Shade pools. Boot prints. Tadpoles. Reed beds. Shallows. Eddies. Snags. Cottonmouths. Cobwebs.

JULY 2

The stare stares behind-the-back, bright, between butt-crack and thigh. The stare widens into a paddle, wide and flat enough to make a draft when it flaps. The stare picks its nose. The stare halfway wonders why the closet door is only half-closed.

* * *

When ecstasy is parted from its practice, when rapture is forced to choose, that's me: the first efforts, independent principalities.

JULY 3

If I draw a hand, say, or a foot, I tow it into view. If I name, a slender ankle, a napping neck, I pull it like a dove out of a derby, pigeon out of a porkpie hat.

JULY 4

"I snuck in through the cellar, through the old coal-chute under the kitchen porch, up the servant's stair (first floor, second floor, third) through an unlatched door into a long windowless hall, past the butler's quarters, the maid's, the cook's, into the attic on a set of steps I found at the back of the broom closet where I hid when I heard the slamming doors down on the first floor, the broken vase, the smashed mirror, someone shouting over and over *you fucking no good whore!*

"Cobwebs. Bat droppings. Mothballs. A stack of overturned washtubs. A mound of rolled rugs. Two silver Christmas trees. A butter churn. A mahogany low-boy packed with bathtub booze. Cluster after slowly curing cluster of little rye-field sparrows hung from the rafters in soft brown bunches the size of my ten-year-old head. A pile of steamer trunks and cedar chests and canvas hampers stuffed with odds-'n'-ends: coyote and coon traps, picnic crockery, pie pans, a powder horn, spools of red ribbon, a pony's tack and harness, a brass plumb bob, tins of trout flies, a bowl of glass fruit, plastic wedding cake, a tray of wooden lures, paper shotgun shells, pickle jars, tinsel, bobbins, a green galosh, a wicker creel, the fluke of an iron anchor, reams of fake gold leaf."

JULY 5

How far will we? How delivered is it? How sacked is the middle made? How much is the middle made to include thereafter?

* * *

"It was a slow day—short hop through the valley, up into the pine bluffs, back into the hills—but I was exhausted. Shitty dirt roads.

"He was a regular looking guy. Thick glasses, check shirt. Probably been up drinking all night. Totally unpredictable.

"I remember the clouds the next morning. Tall, top-heavy, bright white."

JULY 6

Both hands may be free but am I bound—by duty, honor, blame, by shame—to esteem and "hold the pole highly"?

As luck warrants, if weather and wind permit, if the sun says *go*, build a front for it. Make a portico.

* * *

A hum, a nod, a dodgeball, maypole, sugarplum, the lever of the merry-go-round, mound of mildewed stove-wood, Dear John letter, can of rusty finishing nails . . . whatever.

JULY 7

Dusk. Crows. Dirt road. Crack of a distant rifle.

JULY 8

Listen for the number; an object, say, in some special location:
Brass ball at tip of tall flagpole.
Red ribbon braided through a prancing pony's twitching tail.

Baseball buried beneath a pile of sunken brush at the bottom of a frozen pond.

Wet hanky waved from open porthole.

Pulled seam unraveling plaid pant cuff.

Shawl unraveling off cold shoulder.

Thumbprint mashed through a pad of mint marmalade into a slice of sourdough toast.

Gilt-rimmed saucer cracked across its face.

* * *

Was it the season? the citizen? the soldier? the girl in the calico dress? that stirred me, urged me on, that possessed me (veins burst, brain a befuddled mess, heart a compressed smear); that dared me to reach for the underripe peach long before it was ready?

Whatever it was, it was the sound that sounded me, yes, but too soon.

JULY 9

"I remember. It was green. A green bench seat we tore out of a deserted pickup we found one summer down an old logging road a couple miles outside The Corners. Flare gun on the floor, shotgun shells in the glove box. Paper ones. Red paper ones. Red and blue."

* * *

Imagine daily waking to your bedside pledge bowl nightly gifted with a palmful of sand—a dainty mound the size of a pudding cup—instead of your wish for a ten pound ham.

Imagine daily discovering the tail of every arrow on the signpost at the crossroads transformed into a second head.

JULY 10

The method of *loci* is a means of memorization whereby an orator imagines the divisions of his speech affixed to the features of a familiar building, or familiar sequence or group of buildings—head of *exordium*, say, pasted onto the east-facing gable of his stonework country cottage, tail nailed to the gate of the goat pen, *partitio* placed in the form of a series of doormats one atop every set of front steps facing an oft-trodden street—so that his speech (a petition for funds before the senate, a plea before an obdurate judge for his own release) is delivered merely by means of a mental meandering between the plum trees and rose beds beside his own humble home, or a leisurely but equally fanciful stroll down to the end of his mysteriously decapitated sweetheart's cobbled canal street.

Let's say I remember a scene ("midday from balcony") in the form of a frieze ("there a thatch heap, there a filly paddock, a canebrake, ox teams, tree-lined byways, post coaches, hay carts, livery drays, brushwood-bent isolatoes, a decaying mansion, mounds of mildewed stove-wood, a vine-skewered fountain, toppled hitching post, stunted pines, rotting hedgerows, tipped buggy, buckled porticos, peeling stucco, sheared granite, chipped tile") and the frieze is trimmed with silks and satins, the bench beneath it draped with braided laurels and garlands of bay; and let's suppose the trinkets, the festoons, the treats (the offerings of wildflowers, lilies, poppies, perfumed teas, little wreaths of lavender laid along the wall, the brass phalluses, the iron fists, tin horseheads, wax figurines, the sweetmeats and seed cakes and salted fishes and loaves of rye, the squares of linen and scraps of lace) view me as a memory made by wandering the surrounding maze of branching rooms, each with its own frieze, but also form the long curved cone of the hive that shapes—and is where I place when I leave, in the warmth of its deep flaky folds—my memory of the scene.

Okay. But even if I swap a vast expanse of sand for the tidy step-and-rail of Main Street, a frontispiece for a decorative display dish, lateral emphasis for repeated biting, lasting length for point-of-entry, steepness for passage, tilt for duration, state for frame, the mirage of *endless depth* for the effect of *swiftness swept*, a parapet for an observation deck, an actual view for peppery specks, even if I knit the lines tight as playground rhymes and skip to the *swick-swick-swick* of the knot in the jump rope nicking a bump in the blacktop, "the method" is still THE METHOD, and MINE is still "mine"—in that cheap, hissy-fit of a way you've heard it all before: *mine.*

JULY 11

"There were three full bags in the bed of the truck—five, six more in the front seat.

"Terrible son-of-a-bitch knocking, sputtering. It just quit.

"It was so still, so suddenly quiet, I could hear the choir in Paradise Tabernacle on the other side of the hill. I could hear all the way down to the old mill—kids on dirt-bikes; kids shouting, shooting guns."

JULY 12

The problem projected ("diseased laurel losing a leaf") is the problem connected ("an open bosom and a deep chest"); the problem rejected ("a bounce too bouncy") is the problem cathected ("whatever I heard I attempted"); the problem dissected ("*colore* quarreling with *disegno*") is the problem corrected ("*the sliding* bickering with *the beaming*") . . . but for the last time, *where*?

JULY 13

He's delighted. She's indifferent. He neglects. She dissembles. He ignores. She regrets. They forget how happily they forswore one another while turning in place.

* * *

I'll take my views soft and belled, or flared if flat. Wide but not loose. Later rather than soon.

JULY 14

"The grounds? There was the big house and the outbuildings, of course, a smoke shack, a pigeon coop, horse stables, a croquet yard, clay tennis courts, apple orchard, kitchen garden, the little cemetery overgrown with crabgrass, the ragged strips of coconut nailed to broken broomsticks—a gauntlet of homemade bird lures.

"After the hired hands trapped them—sparrows, meadow larks, finches, starlings—they gassed them in the garage with car exhaust. They said she rigged it with mics, recorders. Said she'd rather listen than watch."

JULY 15

Wheat fields, tableland barrows, fog squalls, narrow defiles, junipers, cottonwoods, piñons, sage flats.

Moonlight. A little glade in an almond grove screened by a thicket of forsythia. Hiked half-shirt, dropped drawers, short skirt pushed up. A teenster taken from behind over an old stump.

* * *

Let's take a look at *later*, at *possible*, at *possibly much later.* Let's take a look at *the finished*: if it shows a series of "nexts" succumbing to a foregone foregoingness then the lesson is to never lessen (the profile, say—never swivel it "slightly away"); to never turn from intention but to always see more than the path of cut grass.

Two lines of nine stand face-to-face. The following moves are made, three moves per each in each line of nine—sit, turn, squat, skip, flip, stand, twirl, hop, kneel, twist, sit, twirl, skip, squat, stoop, stretch, jog, jump, bend, hop, stoop, kneel, sit, twirl, stand, clap, flip, leap, stretch, jog, twist, bend, stand, clap, kneel, twist, turn, squat, leap, stretch, jog, run, jump, turn, stoop, jump, run, clap, hop, bend, hop, run, skip, flip, leap—until it ends when they settle anew into two lines of nine.

some off-light (i)

> The relations are those
> of an actual ruin; what falls
> apart, what seems striking
>
> in a single view: a group
> of red sumacs . . . an earliest
> stage of stone wall . . .
>
> a brass bowler broken from its
> trophy . . . a cracked crapper
> plugged with a soggy softball.
>
> "Together" is what the finish
> lacks—*the complete field* crowded
> onto a common route, bent
>
> on a common end (ribbon
> snapped with outstretched
> chest), not just *the complete*
>
> *set* loose in a long flat box,
> bunched in a velvet bag.
> A note, then—the sounded

            or written—is an apart still
a part, a drip looking for a drain
            to dribble back into its leaky

pipe through. So for *influence*
            and so for *selection*. My first
impression: "Too soon." My

            second: "An awfully odd duck
must've picked the particulars."
            My third: "There was accord,

of course, but by main force
            made"—as if rival beachcombers
were told to comb their beach

            arm-in-arm, as if audiences
listened, yes, alert, engrossed,
            immersed, but were obliged

to listen for THE EXCUSE: *arrested*
            at the age of sixteen, the sole
survivor of an overturned rowboat;

friends early and late (coal
heavers, coachmen, deck
            hands, loggers, camp cooks,

porters, millwrights, pressmen);
            a fateful dinner on a wobbly
bar stool; faked phone calls;

            episode at willow grove; trixie,
dinah, donna, dolores; early
            struggles give way to smooth

but troubled sailing, to darkening
            moods, mysterious maladies,
to a gloom so complete not even

            weekly bouts of "make-believe"
relieve the deepening malice.
            My grin grows, ear-to-thrilled-

ear, even though, or so I claim,
            every attempt was botched before
it was even made. Wouldn't

some off-light (ii)

you say OPENING is the real
topic? Is the real topic why
was the land? Was the land

the feeling that the so-called
problems are little more
than a chronicle of accounts

and books cooked, that "no"
was never written exactly?
Was "never" written exactly

by what could be meant?
What could be meant by which
chief traits? Which chief

traits were which *what* brought
up when the ground
was pounded flat on its back?

When was the *where* when
which *what* were the *when*?
How was the ground pounded

down? Who *were* do you
think? Do you think means
                  to make? What faults are

these? Faults enough. If a design
                  is a note—a sound sounded,
a sound sounded for the missing—

                  its key is a relief. I let myself in
with it. Example: working
                  alone, night after night, month

after dreary month, hounded
                  by my own method like a hare
by a pack of barking beagles,

                  I'm assigned by "working"
the essentials of a hound
                  itself. i.e., I chase. And as if

between those who dig and dig
                              and those who merely
mention I burro back and forth,

                    the activity is a listing—of a part
of the apart still a part, of
                    a complete fantasy of a complete

list. In the end the humor
                    was humid, we hoped, if shorn
to a stump; the wait juicy

                    wet as a pull on a leaky pump;
the race thrilling, yes, if there
                    was one *but as fixed as doped*

dogs on a dirt track; the "how" how
                    different, "gimmick" how
gimmicked; the so-called "business"

                    thriving, sure . . . *blossoming, easy,*
breezy, sunkist, rolling in it,
                    carefree . . . but go gentle: my stalk

splits, my coffers gush, troughs
                    dry, unfinished furrows fill.
He's hampered by his own heat.

Two lines of nine stand face-to-face. First-three-from-right and first-three-from-left approach, circle, whisper, coo, nudge, nuzzle, caress, pair off and exit in lewd embraces, reemerge moments later merrily arm-in-arm—spent, mussed, flush-faced. Then the second three pairs have a go, then the third, until it ends when two lines of nine stand face-to-face.

daybook

JULY 17

Thunderheads. Three birch saplings. Three lean-tos thatched with rushes and marsh grass. A bundle of burlap. Three willow withes. Three twigs snapped in half. Thunderclap.

JULY 18

"He slipped into town thirty years ago, MR. B, forever sipping at a weak hock and seltzer, forever washing his linens and darning his woolens and patching his frayed tweeds; forever emptying his overflowing dustbins into the ravine behind the old stone house where for three decades, in a quiet, leafy little tree-lined *cul de sac*, at the end of a long cobbled drive behind a low stone wall and the peeling paint of a pair of black iron gates, he played host and master of revels to an endless circus of crackpots, cranks and oddballs: MR. T, conceited prick of a dandy incessantly twaddling his thumbs, his high-class bitch of a wife and the housemaid with their hands down each other's panties in the pantry—MRS. O after breakfast asleep in a rocker (torn shirt sleeves, fallen socks, split skirt seams)—MISS W shrinking through the shadows with a shaving mug and a bottle of spiced rum—MR. N retching into a dog dish after he shot his toy terrier for eating its own shit."

JULY 19

The fist will bind. The foot, delay. The head, chime. The cap caps like the crown of a tall pine.

* * *

I take heart, I draw hope, from little more than two stick figures on a stick bench embracing in the shade of a stick tree under a sun with five yellow fins.

JULY 20

I owe my deepest debts to Piranesi's intricately exhaustive etchings of the engineering of the emissarium at Lake Albano, to his elaborate reconstructions in the *dell'Acqua Giulia* of an ingenious system of Roman fountains, to his grand *vedute*: the inflated scales, the trick lighting, overcooked details, ready-made moods; the frenzy of cross sections, ground plans, elevations, maps and blow-ups and cutaways and exploded views impersonating the remains of a mosaic floor or the fragments of a ruined fresco, a leaf of parchment or a little placard (tacked to half-open door, garden bench, table leg, suspended from a spike in a fallen *fornix*, a peg in the lintel of a rustic *porta*), but most of all the debt is owed to a shattered slab of marble or a turned paving stone . . . stump of collapsed column . . . the snout of a crumbled corbel . . . the corner of a fractured cornice emerging from a carefully placed pile of Roman rubble only to cross *just so* the frame of the carefully composed view and cast into heavily hatched shadow the accompanying caption.

JULY 21

Tuesday night. Wind. Rain.

JULY 22

Even if anguished, fearful, dejected, regretful, homesick, tearful; even if dismal, numb, lonely, sorry, helplessly overrun; even if she worries, suspects, rejects, flounders, blames . . . she should always *stay, decide, say.*

JULY 23

The problem is to hear: how a shortage is made to heed its missing piece; how a shopkeep spots a thief; how a friend counts toward me from the right as I count from the left—a rye harvest, say, sheafed, stacked in a grain shed.

* * *

Maybe the heat should be hottest where the blues and greens are widest and flattest; the view, like glass, blown.

JULY 24

Buttoning a shirt.
Icing a bourbon.
Toweling a filly's frothing flank.

* * *

"francis, you big fat fraidy cat: don't let a little unease dampen the thrill—
don't let a little discomfort, a little dishonest pat, a secret squeeze, ruin the
surprise of the private excitement."

JULY 25

He chews a stalk of wheat, snaps a stick in two, digs a circle in the dirt,
throws an apple at a fencepost, a pebble at a corncrib, kicks a rusty soup can,
swats a horse fly, rubs an elbow, picks a wart, spits.

He's in luck. He's convinced.

* * *

Raked. The lawn is raked. (*Steep*, not *leafless*. Though it's true, it's free of
leaves. They were burnt in a bonfire a month ago.)

JULY 26

"Filled my flask, drove to the edge of town, followed the old post road
along the river, parked in the gravel pullout at the bottom of the big hill. It was
summer, night. A hot night after a heavy rain.

"I went down to the water to think things over. Came to a little clearing, sat
on a big stump, had a drink, listened for a long while to the crickets and night
birds, bullfrogs, the bark of a distant dog. I walked up the hill to the house.

"A twig broom and an old milk canister from the kitchen porch were tan-
gled in a heap at the foot of the porch stairs with a crockpot, a crowbar, a
couch cushion and the screen door. It was quiet. Lights on, but quiet.

"The kitchen was a shambles: overturned chairs, broken plates, bloodstains
(footprints, boot prints, handprints, smears), a bloody curtain pulled from a
bloody curtain rod.

"In the middle of the main hall one end of a long lamp cord was tied to the
leg of an antique sideboard, the other end knotted in a small loop like a tether
just out of reach of a brass hat stand. The full-length mirror from the foyer was
propped against the arm of a love seat in the sitting room; beside it, a shattered
vase. The front door, in splinters."

JULY 27

Three days of regret and bliss and shame, three days straight, ears full of
a monophone drone: *near to, gone, flared, swollen, shiny, oblong, tiny, faded,
square.*

"To us kids it was all gangsters and flappers and bootleggers, hookers with sequined dresses and pillbox hats. Murder, bank robbing, backstabbing."

* * *

May "the way up" be found—half turned, poor thing, against itself, burnt in its own oven, spent, soused even, pouting, spouting nonsense . . . but found.

JULY 28

What if I "make fast the mizzens and jibs, tar the hull, polish the brass, true the tiller and bail the bilge, send the booms, mend the mainsail, caulk every porthole and cork every crack" but despite my most careful efforts the seldom seen "sixth finger" pokes a hole through my unsuspecting back?

The problem isn't *how*—to properly revere, say, or merely notice or note. *Look! Giotto's gold dust halos!* serves laudably but so does sniffing a rotten egg through the louvers of a locked pantry door.

The key, the crux, is to move into the only open mortise and precisely from that point—the center aisle of the most crowded coliseum on the most central isle in the most turbulent expanse of the deepest and greenest sea of this, our perpetually muddled middle, where the good and the bad mingle freely, words, selves, salvations, devotions, dooms, where they greet and shade and smear—a line breaks its measured pace, is THE FOUNDING of countless far-flung towns, lands, bulwarks, culverts; a gambit bark-peel-by-bark-peel replacing the birch of the canoe it kneels in by preserving its paddler as a fiction.

JULY 29

"A wooden phone booth in the foyer next to a gumball and peanut machine, a few tiny tables through the double doors. A long window seat, dome hockey, a horseshoe bar with a brass foot rail and a giant jar of pickled eggs. TAP BEER—FREE 'TIL YOU PEE written in fat black marker across the lid of an open cigar box.

"*R-r-reee. R-r-reee. R-r-reee.* Squeaky kitchen fan in need of grease."

JULY 30

If "looking" is made to feel certain it's larger than the largest enlargement, "direction" is an accident—and "by accident" exposed as nothing more than a meandering wedge anxiously propping open even the least loose door.

If the call is for a guarantee of the roundness of the ball, the evenness of the sprawl, I can't just say *wait there on the stoop, I'll prove it to you*. I can't just say *I see it all coming*—two tulip-shaped pools of shade shading a single seat, a little bench in a formal garden (*it's hot today!*)—and then say *it was only the seat that'd shifted, not the shade*.

* * *

White cork bobbing in a pool of brandy at the bottom of a crystal snifter. White wicker bench. Line of laundry. Meshed playpen. Closet door swelled shut. Reek of rabbit guts. Hired hand snoring on a grassy bank, drunk brother kicking his drunk knee.

A perfect circle of twenty-seven hillside acres surrounded by a perfect circle of fallow hay-fields and sloping clover meadows.

JULY 31

May the little pantomimes live long, hard and free. May the darkness sleep so deep the light of day never sees the whites of its eyes.

three

rondo

1. for everything, even the most flagrant fountaining, the most congested digression,
2. we're coaxed into believing we ought not to live with—a breach in the bulkhead,
3. *by pen* is to *make by spell* . . . but it needn't be shaped like three acts of a traveling

1. the merest of mere illustrations, the slightest of slender confections—every crooked
2. break in the stem, a clear-cut mismatch we're persuaded to smear into an illegibly
3. tent show (the top to propose, crown to expose, the tail to enclose) or rolled into

1. branch of every bewitchingly bushy branchingness perverting the pen of the poor
2. muddy mess to patch the unpatchable hole in our utterly helpless heads—but
3. a magical fog of predictable props (skinned, stretched, strung—posed as harmless

1. fool unwise enough to indulge himself, or so it's said—because each is also a way
2. it's the unsplinted splits, unplugged breaches, unbandaged breaks, the festering
3. knickknacks) bemisting the funny fact the world they pretend to hide isn't there;

1. to convene, a way to align, each is an *each tuned*: how twilight unwraps a room—
2. mismatches, the accidental in-betweens where everything comes *already sprung*
3. it needn't be recited A-to-Z, no (I hacked it into little pieces, pickled and repacked

1. in crushed tones, in darkening rhythms of little inwardly kerned coves; how my
2. that allow *the imagined* to plop into place alongside *the actual*; as when a fiction
3. it—M-to-Z, L-to-A), even if it means the keys and the key joints (the key guesses,

1. silly dream of the seeping surf says time still has time at its other end, is a fat old
2. suddenly floods the void formed by an innocent misjudgment . . . as when, from
3. key cues, the key cairns) don't agree as foreseen, even if it means I'm on my way

1. dachshund asleep in the grass; how my memory returns to me through an open
2. a tricky vantage, say, *nearby* is mistaken for *middle-distant of a different kind*:
3. to slipping up, so what: while I'm slipping let's let it slide but keep kicking its can

1. window on the main landing of the grand staircase scene by translucent scene:
2. a rag beneath a bush in the backyard for a dog on a hill digging a hole; snack
3. and tanning its hide because if to STOP is to picture and to project—in-the-round,

1. the screened gazebo, the garden shed, shattered greenhouse, the scattered tiles
2. cake wrappers, paper cups, paper bags, bottle caps collecting in a soggy culvert
3. in full perspective—to *plunk* in lieu of *place*, in place of *entering with*, if to STOP

1. of the veranda's ruined roof, the plugged fountain, grown-over gap in the old
2. for rubies and opals and sapphires silted from a swollen creek; a tin windcock
3. is to block every unpleasant perplexity, cork every quandary of *figure and ground*,

1. fieldstone fence, the little orchard with its rotten pear trees and plums, the thickets
2. for a boy climbing a tall tree; deserted filling station for weedy baseball lot; Rotary
3. interrupt every last muddle of missing the melon for its patch, if to STOP is to rest

1. of thorn apple, lilac, Jimson, holly . . . a sleepless night, summer sunrise, a lonely
2. for Moose Lodge; empty saloon for tumbledown towing garage; a note taped
3. where it's heated, dry, well-lit, learnable, where the *why* is just another unsteady

1. stroll down a long-forgotten footpath past the long-forgotten family plot imagining
2. to a bowl of glass fruit for a kite caught on a broken bough; a silver tabby napping
3. hand on an unsteady hawser, another shrunken head in the group shot, if to STOP

1. windlasses, pulleys, bitts, bollards, capstans hidden below a false lawn, ropes
2. on a tin roof for a mouse gorging on a corncob; backward stares and bratty glares
3. is to stall at the part of the story where *I can't possibly send the letter to my long*

1. rigged to made-for-stage manor house, hills, horizon, dawn—the path I walk
2. for well-wishing; a never ending *here* for a never present *now* . . . careful: *everything*
3. *lost love,* then I'll keep pushing, keep kicking, keep cursing my crooked luck . . .

1. as if lit by footlights, the town I see as if drawn on a backdrop, the tree root I trip
2. *as everything's everything* is known as "error-of-halo," even though, in the end,
3. stumble . . . slip . . . succumb . . . and along the way I'll call it wonderful and wonder

1. over placed like a set dresser's prop—and when I return (shirtless, shoeless, sore
2. it seems there's always something to be said for the inverse of blended contact,
3. what else there is. We know: every saltgreen inlet, every lakeside, lily pond, hot

1. toe, sprained ankle, scratched hand) I stop to stand just so, beside the veranda . . .
2. for the lack of any painterly sense of *fore–back–middle*, for ripples of connecting
3. spring . . . remember the dead dog bleeding in the stream? We know: a line of verse

1. on the lawn . . . under the open window. We know: the sudden shiver she blamed
2. terms, crusts of virtual fact, for depending less on isolable tiers to form a working
3. is an unsewn seam, and by its sowing made to serve. We know: from the working

1. on a step on her grave: "as much a knell as a wind through a grove of willows."
2. system core than on pillowy bands of drifting spores. We know: it's about states
3. hand a good comes, that it should go to its neighbor in need. We know: "little

1. We know: a pale desert sky, long desert dusk, the lazy swing of a lone buzzard,
2. of forestating. We know: the score. We know: sage brush, salt flats, high country
3. cricket francis lives in a warm hole with little blue flowers—hear the *tick-tick*

1. a pair of cotton-puff clouds as crisp as the snap of Sunday linens. We know:
2. bluffs and buttes, the prick of thistles and thorns, roar of a narrow gulch, a quart
3. cricket?—how big is cricket?—cricket is eating his good supper—*s-s-shhhh*—

1. a plea for mercy whispered into a whitened fist. We know: a mud-caked blanket,
2. of gin & juice. We know: the wistful stare of a wistful friend, how he pretends
3. cricket is sleeping." We know: for all its appearance of *thus and so* our bustling

1. a bra, a boot, a bloody rope rotting in a rain-soaked ditch. We know: "my darling
2. to see himself seeing an important series of views. We know: "dear francis: gone
3. little burg is no more than a grassy knoll mired in an endless marsh of maybe. We

1. francis: I advance this to you now, in the midst, to also hear . . . what?—I believe
2. to market (vodka, shortening, cornmeal, KY)—wait here—later we fold laundry,
3. know: even though it seems I've snared a mere sparrow to help raise a ridgepole,

1. *so hard* the nape of my neck itches." We know: we know . . . and so there's a split
2. dust, sweep, bake cupcakes, fuck like a dog and a bitch in heat." We know: to *tell*
3. it all comes down to a pot of ink and a slender reed, a well-made line, a place

Two lines of nine stand face-to-face. Each line assembles into a circle of nine. Each circle circles the other circle once-twice-thrice then scatters and sifts into three circles of six. Every circle circles every other circle once-twice-thrice then divides into two circles of three. The threes now begin their cycle of circling, once-twice-thrice, until it ends when they dissolve and reunite into two lines of nine.

finishing work on the face, left arm and foot

If the method is to freely vary but over a bass as sturdy and thoroughly dressed and
                                        set as a stage, to color-by-number but cut across
the lines—to submit
            to the greatest level
            of deformation permitted
                            but still stay whole—a skit might reconsider

its own role, a stab might be taken (but not at the facts?), a *way* might impersonate
                            a *place*, an *empatchment* act like a scene, a *was*
pass for an *about to*
            be, an *about* be
            about to fake a *kind of way.*
                            Okay. But when it comes to minor moments—

the slander, the gossip, the festering grudges, the gathering doubts—first medley
                            outside a bread shop? second at flower stall?
third at family
            hog farm? fourth
            beside emptied dresser
                            drawers? And the frenzied sex benders too—

the raging profanities, squelched moans, swollen thighs, the muffled cries for help,
the ill-lit hovel, iron cuffs, iron bed, iron bands,
the 4AMs, the sedatives,
the humiliating vows,
demented pledges—oh yes,
confessed (narrowly), but later, when the crush

of the critical moment lessens, when the crowd, the many-bodied-as-one, reappears
to irrigate its key scenes. So to make ends meet,
to set each set-piece,
let's suppose I gather
and hem, tuck and pleat,
tab, pin, fold, trim . . . I cut and baste the book

like a shirt newly clipped from an old bolt of cloth, bait the hook, take it line-and-
sinker (I even stoop to wonder which fork
in the winding road
is the "actual way"),
and am I not (—*presto!*—)
pressed into some peculiar but useful conflux?

The nag wags his finger, "Even so, the tone might curl its nose, bite back, take

a turn towards the too pat, too well-aimed,

the too obviously

doable maid."

Then let's suppose I pore

over police blotters, phone logs, rap sheets, file

photos, mug shots. I comb aptness like bees comb honey, larvae, queen. The nag

snorts, "Honest scrutiny girds even the worst

work. What

seems portentous

and unforgettable at first,

a prick that sticks hard and stays—the dark

hallway, cliff bank, empty car-park, the toilet stall, the vicious name-calling—may

soon go to seed. What's first thought lean,

fresh and plausible—

the barren beach,

the rental coupe, the vacant

flat, high tide, lewd banter, the switched keys—

may soon seem cramped, official, rationed." A mess, oh yes. But if it's not mine,
                                    it's nothing, this homage to the half-finished,
this complete lack
        of clear sky; not
        rampart, not backing, not
                                brace, stave, splint, plinth, spline, not even

the simple frillery of fig leafs and fern fronds, grape vines and potted date palms
                                filling the blanks in a harem full of dozing
concubines pink
        and pleasantly
        plump, just-humped, lost
                                in a froth of sandal thongs, silks and sunlight.

So let's say THE TOWN is as necessary to the permanence of the plot as a pile
                                of rocks, but as answerable to its wildest
whims as a weightless
        vapor; i.e., full of enough
        fakery to make it seem as if
                                our sleepy one-horse hamlet—with its cow

pastures and sheep folds, its riverside homesteads and two-room schoolhouse,

                    plank roads and root cellars, its cooper

and smithy, goat

       pens and smoke

       sheds—is a milky Arcadia

                 magically materializing every morning over

its half-dozen dew-laden hills. Let's say ill-favored youth (*the rat-catcher's cousin*)

                 plays opposite untested privilege (*a languid*

ephebe); that against

       all odds the hero

       reaches back, rights every

                 wrong, drifts from hinterlands to center stage

but forgoes a chance at THE SWAYING—which was the heart, which was the crowd,

                 which was the coin. Let's say prose drives verse

into the valley

       of error by turning

       its flanks like a good Greek

                 phalanx—the villain is a villain because that's

where he sends our hero, into the thick of an unwinnable fight. The poem buckles
                              but refuses to fold, bends but holds its ground,
takes a last stand
            to say what others
            can't; an *object*, not to slow
                              or fix or limit but to preserve and implement

fluxness, and flow, after the end, into wider abundance. I could move with less,
                              yes, and less apparent waste too (a bad *mot*
finally made *juste*,
            moved in disgust
            as far from its bumpkin
                              cousin *apt* as it possibly could) but wouldn't

the strands merely cancel, a blue message in a blue bottle beached on a blue beach?
                              "There's death on my street." In the murky
gloom the crowd
            seems to grow
            from the ground, the body
                              it bends over to bloom back in. On both sides

of the divide (body anchored by its vows, capacities, periodic cessions, ills, fears,
                                     limits, pleasures, crowd to the size and rake
of its make-believe
          crown) voluptuaries
          and indulgents, federalists
                              and prudes each form a tide the other tries

to stem, a pool the other tries to drain dry. To rise, the hero doffs drawers, folds
                              cape, wades in . . . tilts hope, reverses fate.
"As for myself,
          I was a damn fool.
          One hot July I squandered
                              the last of mine—good luck, good fortune,

blind but benign chance—at the far end of B.'s flood basin; past the willow groves
                              and myrtles, the brushweed and briars, past
the overgrown
          drainage ditches,
          the game trails weaving
                              through cottonwood stands and sumac thickets;

past the end of the muddiest, least trodden track, the most crooked, as it worked
                                its winding way up and over a tricky hillside,
through a meadow
       of bluegrass
       and clover, through a little
                     belt of blackberries and buttercups, a little

berm of forsythia and oleander, pointing as if a poison arrow to the prim rows
                           of primrose and pansies beside a break
in the sod at the base
       of a stone veranda,
       to the chair on the lawn,
                   her long legs, long black braids, pursed lips,

cocked head, to the odd look she shot me over the top of an open book, her startled
                     laugh loud enough to circle that damned house
up on that damned
       hill like a bracelet
       cuffing a corpse's wrist."
                 It was a hassle, but it was manageable. Think

"low budget smut" with its flimsy plots and lifeless chitchat, colorless interludes
                                and hokey segues, its clumsy close-ups, dull
finales, dumpy
        sets, heartless
        hand-jobs; the cunning but
                                cheerless variations, the stunning discrepancies,

the numbing repetition without pause or swing or cut. Here's my contribution, here
                                they are—the *if nots*, the *why withs*, the *why
nots*, the *ifs*, the *whos*—
        furry little ferrets
        of verse rooting through
                                your ears. Even so, after all the so-called fixes

(the double valves, frantic workarounds, the last minute patches) is it yet a grab
                                bag, a repertory of interlockable lines; maybe
pacing, maybe
        tint or timing
        or intensity alone dialable
                                for each? Was everything . . . already known?

Two lines of nine call out in chorus ("The line is moving. And if there's more than one, the first to move is always the line behind.") until I pretend the way is wide enough to return me to the end; until I pretend the front is a free pass to the bend in its own back; until I linger long enough to pretend that if less be possible to pretend, I've pretended it.

abecedary

A is for

A little wooden ARROW
knocked from its post
at a fork in a dirt road.

B is for

The BALE of dirty rags, the BLUE CHECK
TABLECLOTH, the BRASS PLUMB BOB buried
beneath a moldy mackintosh at the bottom

of a dusty steamer trunk. The BLUNDERBUSS,
the BOLO, the BUGLE, the BRONZE COWBOY-
ON-A-BRONCO, the Navajo BASKETS, the ship's

BELL, the BEAR HIDE, the BUST OF WILLIAM
TAFT, the antlers of a BULL MOOSE crowding
the walls of a walnut-paneled drawing room.

C is for

The CAW
of the thirsty crow
in the parable

of the pebbles
and the half-
empty pitcher.

The COUGH,
you'll recall, that
started this off.

D is for

The DESPAIR of the despondent lover; the defiant "MY
DEAREST" scribbled in blood on the little yellow card
pinned to the bouquet of delphiniums he decides one

morning to deliver to her door. The DITCH where he hides,
where he wavers, where he falters and cracks in the fading
dawn of the fateful day his fading hopes are finally dashed:

"What if the house is locked? I'm too frightened to knock.
Should I bide my time behind these rocks? Should I slink
my way back home, drink my cowardly cup of hemlock?"

E is for

The little EELSKIN
CLUTCH she carries,
the ERMINE CAPE she

wears with matching
waist-jacket and rabbit-
tufted wrap, grey

goatskin gloves, black
satin choker, powder
blue kerchief and cloche.

F is for

"dear (oh so) fragile FRANCIS: I write this
from a booth at a little roadside lunch counter,
five-table den of loggers, longshoremen, pipe-

fitters, welders . . . wonderful homemade mint
marmalade—I saw you this morning under
the little arrow at the crossroads kicking a clay

trough, log and hatchet in hand (your shirt
and shoes matched, your gloves black, broad
back hunched)—if you must know: my feet

are a fine tribute, my calves watery reeds,
withers a warm bed, nipples castor-colored
(two tiny gumdrops), wrists adequate, tits

modest but boffable—that's how *as if* feels—
still, I'm glad . . . pain only a little—closer-in:
I'm sapless, marrowless, flaccid . . . but my

rind somehow ripe, forlorn fins finally lifted
free—can we cut this pit of blue down to just
a dimple?—have a good week, see you soon."

G is for

GROCERY: *masa*, dried
cornhusks, tomatillos,
paprika, *nopales*, *mole*,

pipian, a stone bowl,
a few threads of saffron,
a row of votive candles

ovaled with the Virgins
of Fatima, Lourdes,
Guadalupe, San Miguel.

H is for

The HEX our hero endures—his heavy
HEART, heavy HEAD, the happy
HAMLET fate forced him to forsake.

I is for

IF.

J is for

A JACKDAW mounting
its mate on the bough
of a budding apple tree.

A JOYLESS HAY RIDE
through a forest of joyless
junipers and jackpines.

A pair of JODHPURS
hidden under the seat
of a junked jalopy.

K is for

A set of house KEYS copied
in secret. An empty bottle
of KIRSCHWASSER, a KNOT

of driftwood, a bended KNEE,
a tipsy KISS beside the keel
of the beached canoe she trips

into over a tree root and cracks
two teeth on. A late-night KNOCK
on the door of a country doctor.

L is for

The longing LOOK
of our lonely
leading lady leaning

on the rotten rail
of a flimsy footbridge;
bent over a lovely

little backyard
brook spitting
at a speckled trout.

M is for

MORNINGS in bed. MUSCLE CARS.
Monthly MUSTER at the marching
grounds. The MAIN DRAG at dawn.

N is for

A NARROW CONFESSION confessed
over a bowl of cold noodles into
the barrel of a nickel-plated .38.

O is for

An OBLONG GAP
in a low stone wall,
an OPEN DOOR

on a kitchen porch,
the same OLD BORING
STORY: an obliging

mistress, long hard
stare, the long odds
of ever getting there.

P is for

Four shallow
sockets PRESSED
into a damp

square of sod
by the stubby feet
of a stiff wooden

chair (dragged
into open air
for an afternoon read).

Q is for

The QUILL of a blue jay fluttering
to the floor of a farmer's toolshed.
A dusty trail, a clump of blackberries,

a covey of QUAIL weathering a mid-
summer windstorm. A bloodied
QUILT burned in a backwoods ditch.

The QUIP that joins the questioner
to her quarry; that leads her like a mat
of reeds out of the deepening quagmire.

R is for

A RAY of sun catching
the blade of a spade
digging a hasty grave.

S is for

A SPOOL of coarse brown
twine on a STEP STOOL
in the corner of a SHABBY

TOOLSHED. The SWAY
of ripe wheat in a billowy
breeze. A can of pine

SAP, COW SHEDS, SPRIGS
of bay, grain SILOS, SALT
MARSHES, SAGE FLATS.

T is for

The daily TUNE—
a daily wish list
of what's needed

to even the daily
score: fuzzy but
stable halo, rigid

but open door, fixed
but fidgety midriff,
long but narrow shore.

U is for

Hard climb
UP
steep hill.

V is for

The flimsy
VENEER
of a "happy

home" veiling
the ugliness
of its rotten

rear: the vanity
of the callous
vixen of a wife,

the venom
of her heartless
husband,

the villainy
of the deadly
viper they

· hire to muck
the horse
stable's stalls.

W is for

The WELTS on her
thighs, the WADDED
TOWELS, WOODEN

TABLE, WOODEN
VISE, the fits of
WEEPING, the whitened

WRISTS . . . we hid
so near we could hear
the *snick-snick* of it.

X is for

The XXXs and OOOs
written in lipstick
beneath the big red

smooch on the brown
paper bag in which
she hands him her

Colt, her house keys,
her left pinky toe and
a can of chipped ham.

Y is for

A YAPPY YORKIE
scratching
at a screen

door, a morning
YAWN, runny
YOLK, a noisy little

YELLOW WARBLER
warbling over
a gray day's dawn.

Z is for

A ZEALOUS PLAN shot
to pieces by a platoon
of zealous practicalities.

THREE is for

A dark street, torn sleeve,
a long streak of bad luck
about to reach its ugly end.

terminal transfer

ONE

Let's say the descriptions concern "description" the way a bawdy fabulist's belabored scrum of unclad bodies ("there a slender redhead, there a big blonde, and there, oh yes, just so, a little brunette") concerns the mishmash of dreamed-up orgies he vows up and down he's besmirched himself in like a wallowing sow: puffed—to one-up, to outbid; a tale taller in its telling but when tilted to examine the thin end of its whittled wedge it unaccountably smears into bas-relief, freezes into a touristy tableau. And was I vexed, oh yes! But I wanted a way, this seemed like one: town—crossroads—willow grove—house-on-hill; a way to *approach* but a way to resist too, the farcical pageantry of "I'm a place," the detachable flatness of THE HISTORICAL PLAQUE, the clinical completeness of the daily briefing, the dull *dit-dot-dash* of a poetry-making telegraph; a way to turn a comedy of blind alleys into a heavenly hymn of sweeping vistas, a brown frown into a garland of goofy grins. I wanted a way in. And the way is what sets breakwaters against bowsprits, reefs against rudders; links "the wink" to a good guess; sees semblance as an "always not yet." Ribboned, flared, flounced, modal(?) *the way* is the way around the wideness. (It's coastal.) TOWN: my master plan, my set-piece designed to strand and beach it. But if the motley many are made to march to the beat of THE PERMANENT, to form a single fact, parade a harmonized path, is the marshaled madeness any less of an elegant emptiness than a drum major's epaulet; is it any less a bright neutral empty nought bordered by tassels and braids? No sir, not me. I wanted the bustle of the midway with its clowns and dart games, bearded ladies and petting zoos, its funnel cakes and dunk tanks, blimps and balloons; the mess of an ill-made jack-in-the-box (*pop!*) that pops itself apart; the pretty pickle of a solution as simple as a ballast of a single stone, or as clear as a little signpost at the crossroads to show you the way, but whose "need" is to say finding the right one isn't always so easy: the right stone to steady the tippy canoe, balance the bobbly rowboat, the right arrow marking the right road— not felled by crafty conspirators, turned by pranksters to point the wrong way.

TWO

Uplands to the south of town slope down and level barely three blocks
from the bulkheads, piers and breakwaters, the rail docks, flotsam and fuel
slicks, the sheet-piling and short wharves that form the town's toy harbor
where the river sometimes rolls so low paddle wheelers and barge tows
churn up sludge from the river bed high spot below the iron footbridge,
its elaborate latticework spattered with baitfish and pigeon scat, its filigreed
welcome arch arched over granite cannons and brass plaques, its marble
apron gathering into its engraved fist the gaggle of cobbled canal streets
converging on the slums beneath it—ninety-six years sidewalked and curbed
in red Medina sandstone miraculously preserved under a thin coat of soot,
oil and ash. The nearby apartment blocks and abandoned merchant lofts
are a nineteenth-century tangle of stone balconies and cast iron catwalks,
derelict gas lamps, rotted wagon ramps and toppled chimney pots piling
into the neighboring service core of printers and binderies, filling stations
and machine shops, wine traders, merchant banks, boarding houses,
small engine repair booths, four-stool taprooms, meat brokers, flower stalls,
peep shows, pool parlors, wholesale furniture dealers; tight, tough little
buildings stewed in a perfume of acetone and drive oil, carbon paper
and creosote, rag water, brake fluid, burnt cotton, burnt cork and cold
cream. A row of 1960s apartment towers caps the line of little hills
to the northeast, their common color scheme dampened to match the mood
of the soot-smudged neighborhood, their façades faced with a patchwork
of pre-cast concrete plates custom-made to echo the efforts of mason-laid
walls, to mimic the effects of age—the clearly articulated, highly integrated,
carefully modulated interiors never ruffled by exceptions to the plan, never
punctured by a wayward window or notched by a need for a better view.
When it opened in the 1880s—down the hill, behind the towers—the town's
new firehouse came fully furnished with an engine, four horses, a horse
washer and groom, a sleigh, a double hayloft, two wagons, five chandeliers,
nine spittoons and a coal-fed furnace designed and built by a local hardware

dealer which heated tap water to boot and banked its excess steam to keep the fire engine under pressure while it sat in its stall. Farther north, compact little patches of uniformly setback, shake shingled, nineteen-teens one-over-one doubles mingle with the elegant brick homes once mandated by an 1850s fire ordinance; the mossy mansards and marble window surrounds, the stonework rosettes and intricate balustrades cheek-by-jowl jostling the earlier red brick churches whose simple steeples and modest bell-towers are still visible from the little gateways and sweeping lawns of the low tract homes to the east; the set-piece segments of split-rail, the ornamental carriage lamps and potted wine butt halves, pansy beds and broken wagon wheels, the decals of cardinals and jays curling off curbside mailboxes girdled by an industrial district lined the length of its Belgian block by-lanes with assembly works and gear factories, canneries and packing plants, brickyards, coke ovens, freight houses, rolling mills, brass-, glass- and ironworks built over the groundsills of the original tanneries and distilleries and timber mills long since razed, long since scrapped for their boilers and forges, their steam-powered saws and copper vats. The complex mash of massings—enormous load bay canopies, mammoth furnace pilings, half-mile monitor roofs, three-story clerestories, massive ice chutes—dwarfs the remains of a nearby rail station, its collapsed awnings and adobe pillars as rudely neglected as the retired roundhouse buttoned over the middle of its still serviceable switchyard; its shunts and sidings littered with mothballed rolling stock (cattle cars, boxcars, grain hoppers, open-top coal cars, flatcars, tankers); track-betweens littered with signal pylons and switch huts, crossbucks and cell towers, coupling pins, gang cars, brake hoses, spike plates. A decommissioned power station spreads across the six acres adjacent, its mezzanine's hoist-points still rigged with repeating sets of block and tackle; its work bay floors and looted tool lockers still a mess of box-hooks and jackstays, rigging cable and pulley wire, angle irons and sand-filled canvas sacks; its vast three-floor window

still backdrops a row of now depowered dynamos and frames at its far end
The Flats: a few stony fields, rusty soup cans, rusty culverts, thistles,
dandelions, fox dens. The only transition to an outer rim of long-forgotten
farmland is a lonely band of barrens dotted with debris: paper napkins,
paper cups, egg shells, plastic jugs, half-buried burlap sacks, empty paint
cans, car batteries, dumped asphalt, sofa cushions, phone books, golf balls,
soiled sheets, fish heads, mufflers, bedpans, popsicle sticks, radiator fans,
grass clippings, cow chips, coyote scat, flattened pie pans, anchovy tins,
asbestos shingles and sheetrock and plywood and plaster and lath, junked
dresser drawers, junked planters and flower flats, one-wheeled tricycles,
plastic spoons, soda caps, pee-stained pillowcases, undershirts, toilet
lids, gum wrappers, bullet-riddled oil drums, treadless tractor tires, tree
trimmings, folding chairs, moth-eaten throw rugs, apple cores, boot soles,
shattered 40s, ditched porn, ripped lampshades, carpet scraps, splintered
apple crates, shell casings, carrot peels, cat scalps, dented freezer doors,
de-handled washtubs, de-stuffed beanie bears, de-topped office desks,
doll heads, bread crusts, pencil stubs, tarpaper shreds, melon rinds, mop
handles, truck fenders, beer bottles, broken broom sticks, ripped jeans,
torched mattresses, cassette decks, stolen handbags, mason jars, rabbit
snares, half-eaten salt licks, soggy blankets, snow pickets, shit-streaked
underwear, spackle buckets, pulled tree stumps, used toilet tissue, dirty
diapers, dish towels, worm-eaten camp shacks, long gone fifths of Nikolai
and Old Grandad. On its way to the flood basin floor and the river's near
shoreline, nothing save an old line of post-and-cord to mark the course,
the unfertile, low-rolling scabland gives way to ingrown irrigation ditches,
flooded slate quarries, sage thickets, juniper stands, patchy bands of scrub
oak, mossy belts of hemlocks, marshy tangles of myrtle grass and cattails,
finally the embanked river rocks they once beat their clothes clean on;
a network of locust groves rising from the forehead of the far shore's bluff-like
brow in a lozenge of forested finality as the river flows north out of county.

THREE

Was the sleight not so slight? Was it spread as widely as an urnful of confetti
tipped into a stiff breeze? Was the book blown apart by its own sneeze?
Are the "freedoms" no better than a rigged lottery, the "folds" merely
shallow creases, the "bundles" thick, yes, but as weak as a paper sack filled
with fried leeks? Did I wander my streets like a lost pup? Was I careful
enough? In the end, I was goat, goad, drover; and GROUND was the road
paved to ruin: ragged, broken, rutted, jagged, muddy, stony, steep, if it were
a shoe I vowed to try on every fantastically shaped shoe I could find (I swore
I'd show just what this man's shoehorn is capable of fitting his foot into)
but a slipper as comfy as a lawn tamped and rolled and trimmed for bowls
I promised I'd never permit. The intent was formal, yes, to complete
a formal account, by number laid, on a table spread for the purpose. Instead
it proved little more than a nexus too big for its plexus. I watched it go
like smoke: up—and out an open window. After all the de-kinking and re-
wrinkling, after the boiling and stewing and pickling, the endless blunders
and deepening doubts, my picture-of-picture proved to be just another
picture; not a method, not a manner, not a handy kitchen gadget or a mad
inventor's adding machine, not a little man with a pipe and cape, monocle,
sideburns, dog-ear cap, eye turned to a stain on a rug, not a *frontis-* awaiting
its *-piece*, not a bank of beakers burbling over their Bunsens or an ottoman
pining for its pawned ivory feet, not a number, not a hoe nor the hardness
of its row. It's just a few trees, say, *a line of maples behind a piebald pony,*
neck bent to a narrow stream. On the opposite bank a barefoot boy leans
against the flank of a big black bull asleep under a budding apple tree (big
brass ring in big pink nose) and watches the neighbor's milkmaid wade through
a clump of rushes to feed her waiting pony—little blue bonnet, white smock,
basket of beets balanced on her little blonde head. For all its licked and pressed
hems, at least it allows scenes to set again. For all its dilemmas and awkward
contortions, what if we're enlivened? For all its goof and padding, the truth
is, the more ready a "use" the grander the excuse for not pressing any further.

finish

the teats of august

Canebrakes, bulrushes, marsh grass, drain paddies, a muddy lane, a ditch, a meadow, a path, a hill, a haystack, a hedge, a gate, a trellis, a slate walk, a cedar, a second hedge, a house, another gate, another path back down to the muddy lane, more meadows, pastures, more marshes, more rushes and reeds. But there was no need for the pitch of the wheel to declare: In what then.—Was.—And who was.—And whom.

Not to fail the objects, you put them together—and to what good? In the case of *appearance* that three are four, in the case of *change* that an *index-of-first* versus *actual, all of, in order* counts the number of ways *me* and *my* borrow the nearest walk through *problem* and in just so many ways alters our opening suite: where the blue upcountry tints recede into the greens of a nearer landscape, where the fade falls to its feet, journey, as non-journey, takes place in the place itself because menaced by what runs alongside it. So it spins, 'round and 'round (a mossy stone turned into the *tink* of two milk pails, a *meow* made into a grassy mound) and so not shown in the same sense as a stone or piece of wood, by the finger—but whoever shows, shows. To sum: If you borrow, you owe. If it's the persuasion, suppose it's above. If it's the handling, in a word, *the handling*, in every assent is it enough?

Folds fall. Springs are sprung. Balls bounce. Traps trip. Sod is laid, busted, cleated into clods. A cup chips. A plate breaks. Seams split. Cuffs wrinkle, straighten. A heel slides into a shoe, hand into pant pocket. Brothers write their brothers, lovers their lovers. A blade is drawn through a lamb's leg. And this is the coin, as the saying is, simply to be a part, to act as the hand or foot would: in a manner, *be moved*. But even in the matter of coin, how we've invented, how many means: the sight, touch, sounding. How few words to say the end. You take what's your own—your bottle and your wallet, the jacket with the broad border.

daybook

I first encountered bird lures constructed from coconut shreds (see July 14) in Graham Greene's *The Confidential Agent* (1939). The small-town British backyard in which the protagonist ("D.") at one point finds himself hiding from the authorities is described thusly,

> He was in a tiny back garden—a few square feet of thin grass, a cinder track, a ragged piece of coconut hanging on a broken brick to attract birds. (Part three, chapter one, "The Last Shot")

rondo

This poem is intended to be read the way a hymn is sung from a hymnal: line 1 continuously from page 51 to page 59, then line 2 likewise, finally 3, then back again to where it all began—a tiger with three tails, the tip of each between its teeth.

". . . hear the *tick-tick* cricket?" etc., is an adaptation of the following from Dorothy Kunhardt's *Pat the Bunny* (New York: Golden Books Pub. Co., 1940): "Hear the tick-tick, Bunny? How big is bunny? Bunny is eating his good supper. Sss-sh! Bunny is sleeping."

This passage comprises the entirety of a six-page book ("Judy's Book") which appears within *Pat the Bunny* in the form of a pop-up, a little book-within-a-book the reader is invited to read along with Judy. Judy, you see, "can read her book." *Can you?* (One is reminded of Harold and his little purple crayon. He, however, much like our protagonist(s) here, *makes* the book in which he appears.)

terminal transfer

The description of the "1960s apartment towers" borrows from Robert Venturi, Denise Scott Brown, and Steven Izenour's classic study of vernacular architecture, *Learning from Las Vegas: The Forgotten Symbolism of Architectural Form* (Cambridge, MA: MIT Press, 1977, rev. edition), specifically the discussion of Paul Rudolph's Crawford Manor compared with the authors' own Guild House. (See p. 91 of the revised edition.)

The second section in particular of this fascinating study ("Ugly and Ordinary Architecture, or the Decorated Shed") lends its spirit to much of the present work.

(See for example, part two of "terminal transfer" and the final paragraph of the July 10 entry of "daybook.")

The description of the "1880s firehouse" borrows from Christopher Brown's application to designate as a City Historic Landmark the building known as Fire Engine #2, Hook and Ladder #9, a firehouse erected in 1875 on the corner of Jersey Street and Plymouth Avenue, Buffalo, NY, and which still stands today,

> Besides the fire engine, the house was equipped with four horses, a sleigh, a wagon and "furnishings." In addition to the standard mechanical items one would consider necessary for an engine house, the furnishings also included seven black walnut bedsteads, twelve black walnut chairs, one centre table, one black walnut table, seven arm chairs, one stair carpet, two Brussels carpets, five chandeliers, and seventeen spittoons. The furniture was provided by Burns & Lombart Furniture Company of 61 E. Seneca Street. . . .
>
> The new fire house boasted several mechanical features which were considered advancements in their day. The building was heated by a Peter Martin Patent Moist Air Furnace manufactured by Hauck & Garono Hardware Dealers at 505 Main Street. Besides heating the house, the furnace also provided hot tap water for the bathroom on the second floor. The bathroom with its hot and cold running water was specifically cited as "one of the noticeably excellent features of the building." An electrical stall door opener was another new technological innovation introduced in the building. William Wait, the first engineer at Engine House #2, invented a way to utilize steam from the building furnace and direct it to the fire engine to keep it ready at all times without having to keep the steamer engine fired. (Submitted November 1997 by Kleinhans Community Association, Fargo Estate Neighborhood Association, and the Preservation Coalition of Erie County)

poets out loud *Prize Winners*

Daneen Wardrop

Cyclorama

Terrence Chiusano

On Generation & Corruption

EDITOR'S PRIZE

Sara Michas-Martin

Gray Matter

Peter Streckfus

Errings

EDITOR'S PRIZE

Amy Sara Carroll

Fannie + Freddie: The Sentimentality of Post–9/11 Pornography

Nicolas Hundley

The Revolver in the Hive

EDITOR'S PRIZE

Julie Choffel

The Hello Delay

Michelle Naka Pierce
Continuous Frieze Bordering Red
EDITOR'S PRIZE

Leslie C. Chang
Things That No Longer Delight Me

Amy Catanzano
Multiversal

Darcie Dennigan
Corinna A-Maying the Apocalypse

Karin Gottshall
Crocus

Jean Gallagher
This Minute

Lee Robinson
Hearsay

Janet Kaplan
The Glazier's Country

Robert Thomas
Door to Door

Julie Sheehan

Thaw

Jennifer Clarvoe

Invisible Tender